奥三河

前田真三写真集

奥三河

前田真三写真集

OKU MIKAWA
Photographed by
SHINZO MAEDA

序・色川大吉　2

奥三河への道・春から夏　4〜39

奥三河—日本の原風景・色川大吉　40

奥三河の山河・秋から冬　44〜91

奥三河略図　92

写真データ　93

あとがき・前田真三　94

Design & Layout:Go Asanuma

序

色川大吉(歴史家)

『ふるさとの四季』から『上高地』まで、この十年間、十冊余りの前田真三さんの写真集をふりかえってみると、『北海道―大地の詩』あたりから、ある地域を限定して深く掘り下げるような作風が認められると思う。

特に今度の作品集は何の変哲もない『奥三河』を取りあげたものだけに、いっそう大胆な作家の新しい意図を感ずる。奥三河は豊川、天竜川水系の奥、南信濃や駿河と境を接する山また山の辺境である。そこには日本一人口の少ない村もあれば、七百年来の神事芸能を伝える花祭りの古俗もある。それほどに近年までは陸の孤島の一つであった。その地に前田さんは、ここ数年、足しげく通われた。なぜであろうか。

私は前田さんの作品集では『出合の瞬間』(1977)に最も強い衝撃を受けた者だが、その時以来、氏の作品には、うつろいやすい自然に対して、瞬間ごとに訣別の思いがこめられているのを感じていた。もう二度と来ないであろう一回性の美の瞬間への、半ば諦念に近い愛惜と別離の情があるように思えていた。氏の作品は対象と主体の一瞬の結合であり、光と魂の結晶の表現であろう。だが、それが形を成すまでの作家の不安と無為と空虚の感覚がどれ程のものであるかを、私自身、今度、奥三河の撮影行に同行させて戴いて感じ入ったものである。

『出合の瞬間』にも『一木一草』にも、研ぎ澄まされた一期一会の精神がある。それが『奥三河』になると、これまでの厳しい自己規制枠をゆるめて、人家や人物をまで風景に包みこむ試みをしている。風景から風土へ、一歩足を踏み出されたのであろうか。

私などは、高度成長の嵐の吹き荒れたこの国では、とうに消滅したと思いこんでいた日本の原風景が、まだ、『奥三河』には現存していることを前田さんに教えられた。また、小さな自然を写された息をのむように美しい作品に接するたびに、「神は細部に宿り給う」ということをしみじみと感じた。それは私たちの物を見る目を洗い直し、変える力を持っている。

前田さんは絵筆の代りに写真で、まことに繊細華麗な日本画を描くことのできる方だが、それは水蒸気に富む日本の風土を生かし、靄や光の匂いを写し取る力量を持っているからである。それでいて前田さんは単純な伝統派ではない。富良野の連作を見ても分るように、現代風景を詩に変えるクールな目の持主でもある。それ故、外国人に対する最良の日本紹介者の一人になっている。奥三河のようなこの国の細部にこそ神が宿っていることを、氏は今度の本でみごとに実証されたと思う。

Daikichi Irokawa (Historian)

Looking back at Shinzo Maeda's photography over the years, I have noticed a definite change in his approach; since his book "Hokkaido—Poetry of the Earth" he has shown a tendency to focus more and more on smaller areas and the details of nature. The tendency is very apparent in this book which introduces the visual splendour of that simple, "ordinary" and yet very beautiful area known as Okumikawa.

Okumikawa is located in northeastern Aichi Prefecture, a high mountain area from which flow the headwaters of the Toyokawa and Tenryu Rivers. Mr. Maeda has made several visits to Okumikawa, and one may wonder what has attracted him to an area which, until quite recently, was very isolated. The answer may lie in the unique character of the area and its people. There we can find a village with the smallest population in all of Japan and there, to this day, the local people celebrate a 700-year-old Hana Matsuri—Shinto Flower Festival. It is an area with charms all its own. Of the many books by Shinzo Maeda, the one that has impressed me most is "The Moment of Encounter." After reading and looking at that book I realized that Maeda's work is an expression of a man's deeply felt farewell to the rapidly vanishing beauty of our natural environment. In his pictures, the photographer seems to reveal a sorrow, almost a sense of resignation, at parting with the beauty that will never return again. To me, Shinzo Maeda's photographs seem to be a momentary union of the man and his subject, a crystallization of light and spirit. The capturing of such moments is a difficult task and one that takes its toll on the photographer. I know this because I spent some time with Mr. Maeda at Okumikawa, and I saw how uneasy, how empty and unfulfilled he seems until that moment when he feels he has captured and brought to life what he is seeking to put on film.

In two of his early works, "The Moment of Encounter" and "A Tree, A Blade of Grass," one can see a refined spirit in Maeda, a desire to grasp and appreciate each meeting with nature, each moment of beauty encountered and then lost, never to recur in our lifetime. And now, in this book, Maeda has gone further and included houses and people in his landscapes, something he has never done before. For the first time, he seems to have stepped out of the landscape and into the world of man.

Until recently I have believed that the typical, rustic landscapes of my country have mostly disappeared, swallowed up by our highly developed civilization. But Shinzo Maeda has shown me that such things still exist in Okumikawa. Moreover, in viewing his breathtaking portrayals of the smaller beauties of nature I have come to sincerely believe that "God dwells in the smallest of things." Those who look at Maeda's pictures find that he has cleansed their eyes and changed their point of view.

Mr. Maeda has the ability to paint beautiful pictures of Japan, but he does so not with brushes but with his camera. Through his artistry, he captures the feel, the very aroma of even such ephemeral things as the light and mist which characterize the atmosphere of this country. But Maeda is not just a skilled traditional photographer; his steady eyes take landscapes and turn them into visual poems. It is such genius that makes him so highly qualified to introduce Japan to the outside world, and foreigners will find through this book that, at least in Okumikawa, Japan is still a land where God and the beauty of nature exist in the smallest places and tiniest things.

奥三河への道 春から夏 SPRING AND SUMMER

奥三河には、二本の国道がおおむね南北に走っている。151号線は豊橋からやや東向きに北上して豊川で東名高速と交叉し、奥三河の核心部を抜けて伊那谷の飯田に至っている。もう一本の257号線は、浜松よりやや西向きに北上して長篠古戦場あたりで151号線と交叉して、木曽谷の恵那方面に通じている。ともにくねくねと谷底の川沿いを走り、峠を越えて行く山里の道である。

春はマンサクに始まり、梅、桃、桜と咲き競い、山里を彩る。蟬しぐれの夏になると、色濃い緑の谷を涼風が吹き抜けて行く。渓流沿いには、鮎を求めて大勢の釣人が集まる。この山里が一番賑う季節でもある。

There are two national roads running from north to south in the Okumikawa district. Route 151 runs from Toyohashi northeast to Toyokawa, crossing the Tomei Expressway and going through the central part of Okumikawa to Iida in the Inadani area. Another, Route 257, comes from Hamamatsu and heads northwest to Nagashino, an old battlefield site. It crosses Route 151 and then goes on to Ena in the Kisodani area. Both national roads are mountain roads winding through river valleys and along mountain ridges.

Spring begins here with a bright display of witch hazel blossoms. Then plum, peach and cherry blossoms add their various colors to the mountain villages. When summer comes, with its choruses of myriad, droning cicadas, cool breezes blow through the rich, green valleys, and along the streams fishermen cast for the sweet, trout-like *ayu*. This is the season when the mountain villages are most alive with visitors.

霧の国道151号線 ◇ 奥三河の道は、谷を縫うように杉林の中を走る。雨上りなどにはよく霧が発生して、さながら水墨画の中を行くような趣きである。東栄町
Route 151 shrouded in mist. The Okumikawa road meanders through the cedar forests of the valley.

マンサクの咲く頃 ◇ マンサクの名は、「まず咲く」という言葉に由来するという。鮮やかな黄褐色の花は、山里に春の来たことをいち早く教えてくれる。設楽町

Witch hazel in bloom. The bright mustard-yellow flowers herald the arrival of spring in the mountain village.

梅咲く木馬路 ◇ 山から木を伐り出すのに使われる木馬路。木材搬出方法の近代化と共にこのような昔ながらの情景を目にすることは、なくなってしまった。鳳来町

Plum tree blossoms brighten an old style logging trail running through the forest slopes.

川辺のミツバツツジ ◇ 野山が新緑に衣替えする頃、雑木林の中や川べりにこの花をよく見かける。春先の花としては艶やかで遠くからもよく目立つ。東栄町

Azaleas by a river bank. Even at a distance, the pink beauty of these early spring flowers is easily recognized.

樹間のミツマタ ◇ この木は湿ったところによく自生している。この写真も仏坂峠に至る川辺で見かけたもので、桧林の中に咲くその風情が良かった。東栄町

Edgeworthia blooming in a cypress woods. These bushes grow wild in the moist soil of the forest floor.

山里の春 ◇ 桃の花は、華やかな中にも清楚な趣きがあって、しみじみと春を感じさせてくれる。山々も春霞の中にかすんでいるのどかな山里の朝。鳳来町

The colors of spring in a mountain village. Fresh peach blossoms tell us spring is here.

田造りの農婦 ◇ 農業機械の普及と共に、このような手造りの田は少なくなってしまった。丹念に仕上げられてゆく田は、正に芸術品とも言えるだろう。東栄町

A farm woman at work in a rice field. Mechanized agriculture is fast replacing this kind of farm labor.

金龍寺のしだれ桜 ◇ 金龍寺は、津具村の中心部にある名刹である。境内にあるしだれ桜の大樹は、朝の光の中に絢爛と咲き誇っていた。津具村

Cherry blossoms in the morning sunlight at Kinryuji temple.

春山のどか ◇ 熊谷家の庭から左前方に見える山。春は桜、秋は紅葉と居ながらにして美しい自然を楽しめるよう、代々これらの木々を守ってきたという。豊根村

The view from the Kumagai's house — a hillside of varied patterns and contrasting colors.

水田に映る ◇ 標高500メートルほどあるここ和市では、桃や桜が咲くのもかなり遅い。もの憂い春の山里の午後、近くの藪で鶯がしきりに鳴いていた。設楽町

Reflections on the surface of a wet rice paddy. Nearby bush warblers broadcast the arrival of spring.

代掻 ◇ 前頁の写真と同じ時に撮ったもので、今しも農夫は、田植え前の代掻作業に余念がない。力強い形で画面に入るのを待ってシャッターを切った。設楽町

Absorbed in his work, a farmer prepares his wet rice paddies for another planting.

ツツジ妖艶 ◇ ほの暗い杉林の中で咲き誇っているこのツツジと出合った時には、しばし見とれてしまった。それは正に妖艶と呼ぶにふさわしかった。豊根村

Azaleas in full bloom. Their quiet beauty contrasts with the darkness of surrounding cedars.

源流に咲く ◇ 豊川の源流である段戸高原本谷川の道沿いの斜面には、シャクナゲの花が散見される。この道は、奥三河の秘境裏谷へと続いている。設楽町

Rhododendron blossoms. Here and there they brighten the hillsides by mountain streams.

田植えの頃 ◇ 長江地区には杉林に囲まれた美しい棚田がある。夕日に映える棚田の光景を狙っていたが、ついに思うような情景に出合わなかった。設楽町

Terraced rice fields. In the midst of the woods, they await the planting of seeds.

茶摘み　◇　天竜川の流域では、切り立った斜面に石垣を築いた茶畑をよく見かける。積み上げられた石垣には、永い間風雪に耐えてきた風格がある。龍山村

Harvesting tea leaves along the stone wall of a steep hillside plantation.

カワサツキ咲く ◇ 豊川の支流宇連川は、ここ湯谷温泉のあたりで美しい川床を見せ、板敷渓谷と呼ばれている。6月下旬、真紅のサツキが川辺を彩る。鳳来町

Azalea blossoms. Bright reds color the banks of the Ure River near Yuya Hot Springs.

奔流岩を嚙む ◇ 豊川の上流本谷川は、水量豊富な美しい渓谷である。馳せ下って行く水の動きを、水際の巨岩の上から広角レンズで狙ってみた。設楽町
A rushing mountain stream bites its way through a spray-filled gorge.

畦に咲く ◇ 耕地の少ないせいだろうか、畦に咲く野花が一層美しく感じられる。ヤブカンゾウ、ホタルブクロ等が咲き乱れる納庫付近の水田地帯。設楽町

Wild flowers provide a touch of beauty along a footpath through the fields.

ヤマユリの小径 ◇ かつては何処にでもあったこのような光景も、今はなかなか見ることが出来なくなってしまった。道端に人知れず咲く野花の風情に心ひかれた。設楽町

A narrow path lined with gold-banded lilies. Such a sight is rarely seen these days.

雨の三河路 ◇ 国道151号と257号とを結ぶいくつかの県道のうち、この仏坂峠の道は、なかなか味わい深い山道で、途中一部が、東海自然歩道となっている。鳳来町

Rain along the Mikawa road, a pleasant route following the Hotokezaka Ridge.

ヤマボウシ咲く　◇　梅雨時の一段と濃さを増した木々の緑の中で、ヤマボウシの白い花は、ひときわ輝いて見えた。新豊根ダム下流の大入渓谷にて。豊根村

Dogwood blossoms. Their white flowers stand out against the rich green leaves of late spring.

清涼寒狭渓 ◇ 豊川の中流は寒狭川と呼ばれていて、夏は鮎釣りなどで賑わう。国道沿いにあるこの滝は、大きなものではないが、奇岩との対照が面白い。鳳来町

A crystalline waterfall in the Kansakei Gorge. In summer *ayu* fishing attracts many anglers to this area.

のびる若竹　◇　杉の多いこの地方であるが、竹林も至る所にある。杉などと共に急斜面に生えている場合が多く、四季を通じ日本的な写真が撮りやすい。津具村

Young bamboo. Cedars are dominant here, but bamboo is found scattered among the other trees.

霧の鳳来寺山 ◇ 奥三河地方で最も知名度の高いのが、この仏法僧で有名な鳳来寺山である。かつては数千の石段を歩いて登ったが、今は自動車道もある。鳳来町
Misty Mt. Horaiji. This, the most famous of the region's peaks, is known as the home of many scops owls.

ホウライユリ咲く ◇ うすいピンク色のササユリが終わると、道端に白い大きなヤマユリが目立つようになる。この地方では、ホウライユリと呼んでいる。設楽町

Gold-banded lilies reach out from the shadows by a traditional stone lantern.

夏の熊谷家 ◇ 風雪に耐えてきたこの家は、何処から見ても風格がある。夏の午後、雲の切間から差し込んだ一条の光に、大屋根は浮かび上がって見えた。豊根村

The Kumagai's house in summer. This fine old house has withstood the winds and snows of many years.

畦のヤマユリ ◇ 三沢地区の一角、田の畦にはヤマユリが重い首を垂れている。草を刈る時にユリを切らぬよう心がけた村人の気持が偲ばれる。豊根村

Wild lilies left to grow along a freshly mowed rice field path.

清流に釣る ◇ 大入川の鮎は愛知県下で最も形が良く、美味だと言われている。解禁と同時に、近在ばかりでなく他県からも大勢の釣り人が集まって来る。豊根村

An angler on the Onyu River, one of many who arrive with the opening of the *ayu* fishing season.

雨後の大入川 ◇ 数日来続いた長雨に、いつもきれいな大入川が珍しく濁っている。前頁の写真とほぼ同じ場所で、逆に下流から上流を写したものである。豊根村

The Onyu River just after a shower. The river has been roiled by a rainy spell.

雲海山並 ◇ 標高1415メートルの茶臼山は、愛知県下の最高峰である。夏の朝、御来光は期待はずれであったが、西側の山並は素晴らしい雲海の上にあった。豊根村

From Mt. Chausu distant ridges loom above clouds and forests that call to mind a traditional ink painting.

谷の通り雨 ◇ 奥三河一帯は、水気の多いところで、この水分が杉桧の成育に役立っている。雨の通りすぎた谷からは、盛んに霧が立ち昇っていた。豊根村

A shower passes through the valley. The humid Okumikawa area is ideal for cedars and cypresses.

谷間の青田 ◇ 手前はこんにゃく畑である。これといって特徴のない場所であるが、これこそ奥三河の風景であり、日本古来の山村のたたずまいと言えるだろう。設楽町

Yellow-green rice paddies, a meandering stream and farmhouses — a typical mountain scene.

畦の草刈り ◇ ここは三沢高原と呼ばれており、夏は民宿などで賑わうところである。草いきれの炎天下、畦の草刈りもひと仕事である。豊根村

Cutting weeds along a rice field path — a hot difficult part of a farmer's life.

夜明けの高原道路 ◇ 茶臼山高原道路は、眺望絶佳な山岳観光有料道路である。面ノ木園地等を抜けて、設楽町の納庫で国道257号と合流している。豊根村
The highland road at dawn. This mountain sightseeing road offers spectacular views for visiting tourists.

村祭りの花火 ◇ 7月下旬、白鳥神社の祭りの日に花火大会がある。散発的に上る花火の合間に、蛍が盛んに飛び交っていた。情緒豊かな山里の夏の夕暮。津具村

Fireworks display at a village festival. A brilliant burst against the soft afterglow left by an earlier rocket.

奥三河―日本の原風景

色川大吉(歴史家)

古来、道は川に沿って川下から川上へと通じていた。近代の道のように幾つもの川を真横に断ち切って海岸線に並行して作られていたわけではない。奥三河の道も豊川に沿って豊橋から東栄に通じており、今ではそこを飯田線が走っている。

日本列島の道はおおむねタテ型で、中央脊梁山脈から流れ落ちる急峻な川に沿って上下していた。だから峠が多く、峠からの眺望や渓谷の美にめぐまれ、また里を結ぶ道の交点に宿場町などを栄えさせていた。

三河から北へは伊那街道や秋葉街道が通じ、そこは物資の流れと共に、豊川稲荷や鳳来寺や長野の善光寺に詣る旅人の往来する道にもなっていた。しかし、北設楽郡を主とする奥三河となると、街道の幹線からもはずれ、江戸末期、飯田町が名古屋方面への陸送で「出馬千匹入馬千匹」と賑わっていたころ、こちらは「馬が山犬(狼)を怖れて痩せる」といわれるほどの淋しさであった(早川孝太郎『三州横山話』)。

その最奥地富山村は中世の落武者が住みついた所といわれ、昭和二十八年には、まだ百九十世帯があったのに、今では七十世帯ほどに激減し、日本一人口の少ない村となっている。隣りの豊根村も最近でこそ自動車道が開通して、茶臼山観光の基地となったが、それ以前は富山村や南信濃の遠山郷にも劣らぬ僻村であった。この山深い豊根から津具村、東栄町にかけての一帯は国の重要民俗文化財に指定された「花まつり」の本場であり、有名だが、これが世に紹介されたのは、わずかに五十年前、地元の民俗学者早川孝太郎の『花祭』の公刊以後のことにすぎない。

早川孝太郎がこの花まつりを初めて見たのは十三歳の時、郷里横山の近く、鳳来寺の門前町門谷であった。その時は野天に湯立の竈を築いて舞われたという。その後、早川の家に榊鬼がやってきて、目の前で悪霊退散のへんべ(足ぶみ)を踏んだ。その怖ろしさが忘れられずに、長じて柳田国男に話したところ、柳田からすすめられて本格的に花まつりの調査に取りかかった。大正末年、折口信夫と同行して二人で豊根村の山内の花まつりを見にゆき、それから憑かれた者のように打ち込んで、ついに昭和五年(1930)、不巧の大著を世に出したのであった。

その早川によると、この中世古来の神事芸能は修験道の影響が濃く、「山伏の一派かと思われる先達によって七年目ごとに三日三夜にわたって神の世界を現出したと伝えられる。」その村々の共同による大神楽の祭りは、安政四年(1857)、今の豊根村字上黒川での行事を最後に中絶してしまい、今の花まつりはその後をひき継いだものだという。

豊根の上黒川といえば、前田真三氏の奥三河取材の基地でもある。氏は上黒川の豪農熊谷賢一氏と親交があり、その別宅を借りて仕事場としていた。前田氏が奥三河を隈なく歩き回れたのは、この友情と拠点があったからでもあろう。熊谷家は江戸末期の代表的な豪農の遺構で、国の重要文

化財にも指定された建築(表紙の家がそれ)だが、当主の賢一氏は惜しくも去年六月に急逝されたのである。

十七世紀の『人国記』に言う。三河人は「偏屈にて我言を先とし、人の述べる処をまたずして是を談じ、命を終るの族多し」と。熊谷家の当主の人となりも、そのようであったと聞く。前田氏はこうした三河人の愚直な奇骨をその山河とあわせて愛したのではないだろうか。私もこの重文の豪農邸に一夜の宿をしていただいて、奥三河の深さと夜の静寂の重さを身に受けとめた。

前田氏も奥多摩の山村(恩方村)に生れ、その自然の中で腕白時代を過している。その体験に基ずく深い洞察が、この写真集には活きているように思える。氏が今度、自分の風景の中に安心して人文的な風物を受け容れているのは、血肉と化している少年期の山村の原像が心を乱すことなくその内部に坐っているからでもあろう。

早川孝太郎の『花祭』の何よりの意義が、日本の辺境といわれた奥三河に久しく埋もれていた田楽、神楽、念仏踊、地芝居等、さまざまな芸能を一挙に掘り起して、このような僻地にも日本の民間祭祀や芸能史を見直させるような鮮烈な民俗、芸能が生きていることを広く知らしめた点にあったとするなら、前田真三氏のこの『奥三河』は、日本の原風景ともいうべき懐かしい姿を、春夏秋冬を通じ、山深い一地域に始めて再現してみせたものとして久遠の価値を持つであろう。

花まつりの神事芸が、「裁着姿に草鞋履きという軽快な姿で、全身を駆使して目まぐるしいまでの動きで、山伏的なにおいが強い」(早川)のに対して、奥三河の自然、風土が、地味で質朴でありながら、野に咲く花のような可憐さをたたえているのは、里人の温かい心の故か、神々のなせる業か。変転止まぬ自然のなかにも明らかな四季の色彩の饗宴があるように、厳冬期の山里の祭りにも、幼年、青年、壮年等の人間成長の季節に即した多くの舞いが作られていた。前田氏のこの写真集は、こうした人間ドラマの「場」を、小さな自然から大きな風景にいたるまで、みごとに捉えて構成されたものといえる。

日本人は古来、山には神が宿り、諸霊がこもるという信仰を持ってきた。その深山幽谷に分け入り、滝に打れ、峻嶮を攀じ、修行を果した者は、霊的能力を身につけ、里人を救う力を備えていると信じられてきた。最初は大和や熊野あたりから参入したであろう修験者たちが、やがて里に定着し、里人と力をあわせて山谷を拓いた時、そこに親しみ深い景観があらわれた。前田真三氏はそれらを知りつくした上で、いったん自然も人間も風物も無常の時のなかにおさめて濾過し、然る後、黙々と写真を撮られたのだと思う。

OKUMIKAWA—WHERE THE OLD JAPAN LIVES ON

Daikichi Irokawa (Historian)

The highways and roads of modern Japan cross rivers and run parallel to the coastline, but in the old days they generally followed the courses of rivers from their lower stretches up to the headwaters. This is the kind of route taken by the roads of Okumikawa, following the Toyokawa River from Toyohashi to Toei, an area now serviced by the Iida Line of the Japanese National Railways.

The old roads which traversed the Japanese archipelago mostly ran lengthwise from north to south along the steep-walled flowing from the central mountain ranges. Along the way there were many mountain passes and gorges which provided and still provide scenes of great beauty. In the old days there were post towns at the crossings along the routes between villages and the roads served various needs of the area. They were not only used by merchants transporting goods, but by travellers and pilgrims visiting such shrines and temples as Toyokawa-Inari Shrine, Horaiji Temple and the great Zenkoji Temple in the city of Nagano. Towns like Iida prospered so much from their trade with the Nagoya area that, according to one account, Kotaro Hayakawa's "Sanshu Yokoyama Banashi," "one thousand horses came and went in the town every day." The Okumikawa area, however, was not on the main route, and its villages were so isolated and wild that it is said that the horses there got skinny worrying about the wolves in the area.

Tomiyama Village, the most isolated in Okumikawa, is said to have been a place of refuge for fugitive warriors during the Feudal Period. Today its claim to distinctionis that it is the village with the smallest population in Japan, and in the last three decades the number of resident families has dropped from 190 to 70. On the other hand, Toyone, a neighboring village which was once as isolated as Tomiyama, is now, thanks to a new highway, a bustling jumping off point for sightseeing around Mount Chausu.

Toyone and the neighboring communities of Tsugu and Toei are well known for their Hana Matsuri—Shinto Flower Festival, which the Japanese Government has designated as an important folklore asset. This festival was first introduced to outsiders only 50 years ago when Kotaro Hayakawa, a local folklorist, published his book "Hana Matsuri." Hayakawa was only 13 when he first saw the festival at Kadoya's Horaiji Temple near his hometown of Yokoyama. He recalls the villagers dancing around a cauldron of boiling water on that occasion. Then, at a later date, a "devil dancer" from the festival came to his home to dispel evil spirits.

He never forgot the fear he felt when he witnessed that dance, and later he mentioned his experience to Kunio Yanagida, a folklorist. Yanagida encouraged him to do more research on the subject and in 1926 Hayakawa and another folklorist, Shinobu Origuchi travelled to Toyone Village to see the festival again. From that day forward, Hayakawa's interest steadily increased until he became almost obsessed with the subject. Finally, four years later, he published his classic work on the festival.

According to Hayakawa, the original form of this Shinto Festival of the Gods, which dates back to medieval times, was very much affected by the asceticism of the local mountain priests. The early villagers, he tells us, appeared much like a group of mountain priests as they celebrated the festival. During the three days and nights of the festival, which was held every seven years, it seemed as if these early participants actually brought to this earth the world of the Gods. The original festival, with its sacred Shinto music and dancing, could still be seen at Kamikurokawa in Toyone Village as late as 1857. After that date, the festival underwent changes and assumed the form in which it is seen today.

Kamikurokawa, in Toyone, became the base for Shinzo Maeda's work in Okumikawa, and the photographer came to know Kenichi Kumagai, a wealthy local farmer who offered Maeda the use of one of his houses. It was through Mr. Kumagai's friendship and assistance that Maeda was able to move about freely in the Okumikawa area. The Kumagai residence, which appears on the cover of this book, was built in a style typical of the homes of wealthy farmers during the late Edo Period. It has been designated as an important national cultural property.

There was a book published in the seventeenth century called "Prefectures and the Character of their People." In this book the people of Okumikawa are described as eccentric, strong-minded people who say what they want to say, without waiting to hear the opinions of others. It adds that they are great talkers. I have heard that Mr. Kumagai fitted that description well, and I have a feeling that it was not only the beauty of nature but the simple, forthright spirit of the local folk that endeared the Okumikawa region to Mr. Maeda's heart. Shinzo Maeda was, himself, born in a mountain village outside of Tokyo and spent his boyhood surrounded by nature. It seems that deep insights gained from the experiences of his youth have come into play in his work on Okumikawa, and it may be that the images which lie undisturbed in the man's mind provide some explanation for Maeda's finally bringing man and his culture into his pictures.

Kotaro Hayakawa's book "Hana Matsuri" appears to have two primary objectives. They are (1) to thoroughly explore and gain an understanding of the religious festivals and ceremonies (Buddhist and Shinto) and the folk drama music and dancing which were buried for so long in the isolation of the Okumikawa area, and (2) to introduce this folklore and religion and encourage people to take a fresh look at the festivals and ceremonies that live on in some of the country's isolated areas. I believe that Shinzo Maeda's "Okumikawa" is a classic supplement to Hayakawa's work, a collection of photographs which open our eyes for the first time to the beauty and charm of the land and people in Japan's mountain districts. As mentioned above, Hayakawa felt that the early Hana Matsuri in some ways resembled the dances performed by the mountain priests. Like the priests, the participants in the Hana Matsuri were clad in light, simple costumes and sandals but danced about in a very lively manner. In contrast, the natural environment in which the villagers lived was plain and quiet, though filled with loveliness. Was this because of the character of the people, because of their love of the land? Or was it a blessing from the Gods? No one knows. But we do know that in every season of the year, the natural beauties of the Okumikawa area are a feast for the eyes, and there are dances for each of the seasons, just as there are dances designed for different age groups, some for children, some for youth and some for older folks.

Ever since ancient times, Japanese people have believed that gods and spirits dwelled in the mountains. Because of this, those who penetrated the land's deep mountains, those who tested themselves by cilmbing lofty peaks and purified themselves beneath icy waterfalls, were thought to possess special spiritual powers and the ability to help village people. And indeed, the mountaineering ascetics, who usually started from the ancient towns of Nara or Kumano often stopped over at villages along the way and helped the local people carve out a living in the rough mountains and valleys. Shinzo Maeda fully captures the essence of the setting for these human sides of Okumikawa as well as the loveliness of nature which can be found in the regions widest landscapes and smallest manifestations of natural beauty. I believe that the process of creating this book furnished him with a deep understanding of Okumikawa, its people, their land and their culture. This he put into some sort of mutable time frame and filtered through his own sensitivity. Then—silently, painstakingly—he captured it all on film, This book is the final and very beautiful result of his efforts.

奥三河の山川 秋から冬 AUTUMN AND WINTER

愛知県東北部の山間地帯奥三河、高くはないが重畳たる山並が続き、山々は杉桧の美林に覆われている。奥三河の中心地愛知県北設楽郡は、その総面積の92パーセントが林野で、農耕地はわずか3.8パーセントに過ぎない。そして森林の70パーセント以上が人工林地である。天竜川水系の大入川、大千瀬川、そして豊川、矢作川等の本支流が、山あいを縫うように流れ、それぞれ美しい渓谷美を競い合う。

秋は、黄金色に輝く田に始まり、杉林の中や川辺に点在する紅葉の饗宴で最高潮に達する。木々が葉を落とし、霜が降るようになると山里も冬仕度である。そして、杉林や渓谷を背景に降る雪は、ひと時、水墨画の世界を演出してくれる。

Okumikawa, a part of northeast Aichi Prefecture, is a region of mountains which, though not impressively high, are covered with beautiful forest of cedar and cypress. The central part of the area, North Shitara County, is mostly forest. Only 3.8 percent of the area is farmland. 92 percent is forested, and of that, seventy percent is the result of reforestation.

The main rivers and branch streams such as the Onyu and the Toyokawa seem to vie for the honor of being most beautiful as they wind through mountain ravines.

Autumn in this area begins with shining golden rice fields. Soon the maples scattered through the cedar forests or along the brooks and streams become a banquet of color as they reach the climax of their seasonal display. Then one day the leaves start to falling and when the first frost appears in the mountain villages, nature and man begin preparations for the winter. Finally, snow falls on the woods, hills and ravines. The landscape resembles the subtle strokes and washes of a traditional ink painting.

秋気澄む ◇ 杉林の中に黄葉の木が一本、この地方で良く見る光景である。折しも秋の斜光を受けて木は鮮明に浮かび上っていた。天竜川河畔にて。佐久間町

A single yellow tree, alone in the dark shades of a cedar forest.

畦の彼岸花 ◇ 彼岸花は、全国一斉に秋の彼岸頃に咲く。豊根あたりでは余り見かけないが、ここ新城あたりでは至る所で田の畦を真赤に染めている。新城市

Cluster amaryllis bordering a rice field. Throughout Japan these blossoms appear around the autumnal equinox.

初秋の風 ◇ 初秋の風物詩であるススキは、何処にでもあるが、この地方には少ない。ここ巴川の川辺のススキは、初秋の光を受けて銀色に輝いていた。作手村

Silver eulalia in the autumn sunlight. Abundant elsewhere, this plant is seldom seen in the Okumikawa area.

野菊秋麗 ◇ 初秋の頃になると、至る所で野菊を見かけるが、このように華やかに咲き誇っているのも珍しい。本宮山スカイラインの道路わきで。作手村

A large and particularly lovely patch of wild chrysanthemums on a slope of Mt. Hongu.

こぼれ咲く萩 ◇ 日本の秋を代表する花はたくさんあるが、この萩もそのひとつである。夏の暑いうちから咲き始め、秋の終りの頃まで咲き続ける。津具村

Japanese bush clovers. These pink flowers bloom from the middle of summer until the end of autumn.

森厳杉林 ◇ 杉木立の中に霧が入った写真を狙っていた。雨が上がった初秋の朝、かねてより見当をつけていた柴石峠付近でその念願を果たした。東栄町

On an early autumn morning, mist follows rain through a solemn stand of cedars.

山間秋天 ◇ 山国奥三河には広い空が少ない。谷底から見上げると、今日は珍しく雄大な白雲が、杉木立の上を悠々と流れ去っていた。冷気立つ秋の朝。豊根村

A chill autumn morning with a great white cloud silently passing above the cedar-covered mountainsides.

朝のみどり湖 ◇ 新豊根ダムによって出現したみどり湖は、水面に杉小立を映して美しい。気温の下がった今朝は、湖面から盛んに靄が立ち昇っていた。豊根村

Morning on Lake Midori. Cedars cast their reflections on the dappled surface of the man-made lake.

山田の小径 ◇ 小さな木橋を渡り、小径は奥へ奥へと通じている。かつては何処にでもあった平凡な風景であるが、これこそ日本の風景の原点であろう。足助町

A path through mountain rice fields. Such scenes have been part of Japan since the olden days.

山間の大地 ◇ 杉林に囲まれた台地の稲田は、秋の陽に黄金色に輝いていた。少々おおげさな題名であるが、ここに立った時の実感である。御園地区で。東栄町

An autumn sun casts golden light on the terraced rice fields between the mountains.

花ノ木模様 ◇ 花ノ木は楓の一種で、愛知県の県木である。新緑も美しいが、黄・橙・紅と染め上げられた紅葉の色模様は、実に鮮やかで独特の美しさがある。津具村

Hananoki, the official tree of Aichi Prefecture. Here it is alive with a pattern of brilliant autumn colors.

路傍の千草 ◇ 自然は時として道端に素晴らしい贈物をばらまいてくれる。仔細に見ると、土手の千草は夜来の露を宿して、美しい絵模様を作り出していた。豊根村
Roadside plants glistening with the extra beauty added by the morning dew.

秋深し ◇ 秋になると、山里のあちこちで焚火の煙が上がる。焚火の煙はなぜか人々を感傷的にさせる。それは、ゆく秋を惜しむ日本人の心かもしれない。豊根村

The smoke of an autumn bonfire brings, for Japanese, melancholy thoughts of the season's end.

朝露の中に　◇　奥三河の出入りによく通る新野の朝である。取入れも間近い9月の下旬頃、折からの朝露に鴉が二羽、シルエットとなって浮かび上がっていた。阿南町

Two crows perch, silhouetted against the mist of a late September morning.

光る天竜川　◇　佐久間ダムよりやや下流のこの付近も、両岸は杉の人工林で覆われている。秋の日に光る川辺には、釣人がのんびり糸を垂れていた。佐久間町
An autumn day on the glistening Tenryu River with fishermen quietly enjoying their sport.

立昇る光 ◇ 御来光を狙って茶臼山にたびたび足を運ぶが、なかなか良い条件に恵まれない。しかし、このような幸運に出合い、天の贈物に感謝することもある。豊根村

Unexpected beauty glimpsed from a mountain top. A rising sun casts its rays through the morning mists.

川辺に燃える ◇ 奥三河の山は大半が杉桧であるから、全山紅葉という景観はない。しかし、川辺にもみじが多く、渓流と組み合わせた写真が撮りやすい。豊根村

Maples above a mountain stream. Such splashes of brilliance appear here and there among the evergreens.

秋の寒狭川 ◇ 川岸の鮮やかな紅葉は、秋の陽に光り輝いていた。紅葉と水とススキと青い杉林との取り合わせは、この地方ならではのものである。設楽町

Autumn along the Kansa River. Green cedars and silvery rushes give the area a special loveliness.

もみじあでやか ◇ 柔らかな秋の日ざしを浴びて、真赤に色づいたもみじはひときわ鮮やかだ。ボケ味の良いレンズを使って、その豪華な衣裳を再現してみた。鳳来町

Delicate maple leaves. The beauty of the bright reds and oranges is heightened by the soft autumn sun.

友禅模様 ◇ ムラサキシキブは、秋の実のなる季節以外は余り目立たない。木々の紅葉の中で見たこの実は、さながら友禅模様のような美しさであった。津具村

Purple berries and green leaves. The shrub Lady Murasaki sometimes resembles a lovely pattern of printed silk.

花ノ木紅葉 ◇ 茶臼山の登り口にある川宇連神社の境内には、花ノ木の自然林がある。自生しているものは非常に珍しく、国の天然記念物に指定されている。豊根村

Bright *hananoki* leaves. Aged specimens of this tree are often designated as national treasures.

錦秋絵巻 ◇ 杉や樅の針葉樹に混じって、もみじが絢爛たる錦絵を見せている。13ページの「春山のどか」と同じく熊谷家の庭先から写したものである。豊根村

A hillside of mixed maples cherries, and evergreens, their forms and colors like a natural woodblock print.

輝く珠玉 ◇ 柿と田圃の取合わせは、秋の農村風景の代表的なものである。ここ長江の棚田で出合ったこの光景は、正に珠玉輝くといった感じであった。設楽町
A dazzling spray of persimmons by a rice paddy. This is a typical farm village landscape.

雨後の山里 ◇ 信州の伊那谷あたりは、同じ山村でも何となく風景が乾いている。奥三河の特徴は、水気を含んでいて風景がしっとりしていることであろう。東栄町

After a rainfall. A soft, wet feeling permeates the Okumikawa landscape.

刈田の印象 ◇ これから稲架に掛けられるのだろう、稲束が田に敷きつめられていた。稲の一粒一粒を克明に描写しようと超大型カメラを取り出した。稲武町

Sheaves of rice, waiting to be hung and dried, form a pleasing design on the cool fields.

晩秋夕暮 ◇ 取り入れの終わった作物の殻を火にくべる農婦。日が沈むと急に冷え込んできたが、赤々と燃える火は、言いようのない温もりを感じさせた。津具村

The crop harvested, a farm woman burns rice husks in the late autumn twilight.

土蔵の印象 ◇ 白と黒に塗り分けられた熊谷家の土蔵の壁である。古典的な中にも、不思議とモダンな感じがある。そのシンプルな美しさに心うたれた。豊根村

The black and white of a traditional storehouse wall appears classic and yet somehow modern.

秋の熊谷家 ◇ 晩秋の日ざしに土蔵の壁の白さが眩しい。様々な角度からこの家を撮ってきたが、今日は思いきり近づいて、画面一杯に取り込んでみた。豊根村

The Kumagai's house in autumn, its white-walls dazzling in the bright sunlight.

山並遥か ◇ 茶臼山から見た南アルプス南部の景観で、荒川、赤石、聖等の山々である。良く晴れた日には、遠く仙丈、白根三山などを望むこともできる。豊根村

A mountain panorama. In the distance, Mt. Akaishi and other peaks of Japan's Southern Alps.

秋の日だまり ◇ 峠をひとつ越えた信州の飯田あたりは干柿の産地として有名だが、この付近では時折農家の軒先などで見かける程度である。設楽町

Patterns in the autumn sunlight. Persimmons drying under the eaves of a farmhouse.

路傍の石仏 ◇ 奥三河地方を歩いていると、道端によく石仏を見かける。それは大小さまざまであるが、いずれも柔和な眼差しで旅人を見つめている。設楽町

A roadside Buddhist image. Whether small or large, these stone carvings all gaze gently at passing travellers.

落葉の渓谷 ◇ 風が吹くたびに散るもみじ。あるものは水の流れに吸い込まれ、また、あるものは岩の上でしばし秋の名残りをとどめる。鳴沢の滝付近にて。作手村
A silvery stream flows swiftly between dark rocks strewn with windblown maple leaves.

霜柱の朝 ◇ 今朝はずい分冷え込んだと思ったら、一面の霜柱である。よく見ると落葉が一葉霜柱に持ち上げられていた。冬も間近い茶臼山で。豊根村

Morning frost. Crisp columns of frost lift a jewel-like leaf from the forest floor.

落葉の山路 ◇ 奥三河地方には雑木の山が少ないので、この写真のような山路になかなか出合わない。この写真は、長江地区の棚田の下部で撮影したものである。設楽町

A leaf-carpeted path through one of the few mixed hardwood forests of the Okumikawa area.

疎林新雪 ◇ 夜来の初雪に疎林はうっすらと雪化粧をしている。初冬の頃の山里は一年のうちで最も物寂しい。しかし、この寂しい光景もまたいい。根羽村

Fresh snow on a sparsely wooded mountainside. It is early winter, the loneliest season in the mountain villages.

霏々として降る ◇ 平野部の新城あたりが雨の時でも、山間部のこの付近は雪のことが多い。この日は、朝から猛吹雪で横なぐりの雪が終日降り続いた。豊根村

A driving mountain snowstorm. Such storms may start in the morning and last all day.

薄雪の茶畑 ◇ お茶はこの地方の特産品のひとつである。今日は珍しく茶畑に雪が降った。地味な冬の茶畑が一変して、面白い造型美を見せてくれた。東栄町

A tea plantation powdered with snow, transforming a drab winter scene into a natural art form.

新雪杉林 ◇ 冬の最も奥三河らしい写真をこの面ノ木付近で捉えることができた。うっすらと杉林に付着した雪は、厳しい寒さに霧氷状に凍りついていた。稲武町

A cedar forest draped with fresh, frozen snow, clinging like hoarfrost on the frigid branches.

雪降る熊谷家 ◇ 重厚な茅葺き屋根の民家は、本当に少なくなってしまった。杉林を背景に降りしきる雪の中に見るこの光景は、正に日本の風景である。豊根村

The Kumagai's house. Its beauty is set against a background of snow and cedar woods.

凍るみどり湖 ◇ ここは雪は多くはないが、寒さは厳しく、このみどり湖もよく結氷する。凍った湖も美しいが、音を立てて割れてゆく時もまた面白い。豊根村

Lake Midori. The frozen lake's picture-like beauty will last even after the ice starts cracking up.

天狗棚霧氷 ◇ 津具の平から見上げると、面ノ木あたりの樹林が白く望見された。見事な霧氷とまではいかなかったが、念願の一枚をものにした。津具村

The silver thaw at Tengudana. Light and shadow on a lacy winter landscape.

雪の坂宇場川 ◇ 昨日一日降り続いた雪も、今朝は見事に晴れ上がった。石の上に積もった雪が、朝の柔らかい日差しを受けて、清浄な美しさを見せていた。豊根村

Snow-covered rocks in the Sakauba River. Mounds of pure white glistening in the soft morning sun.

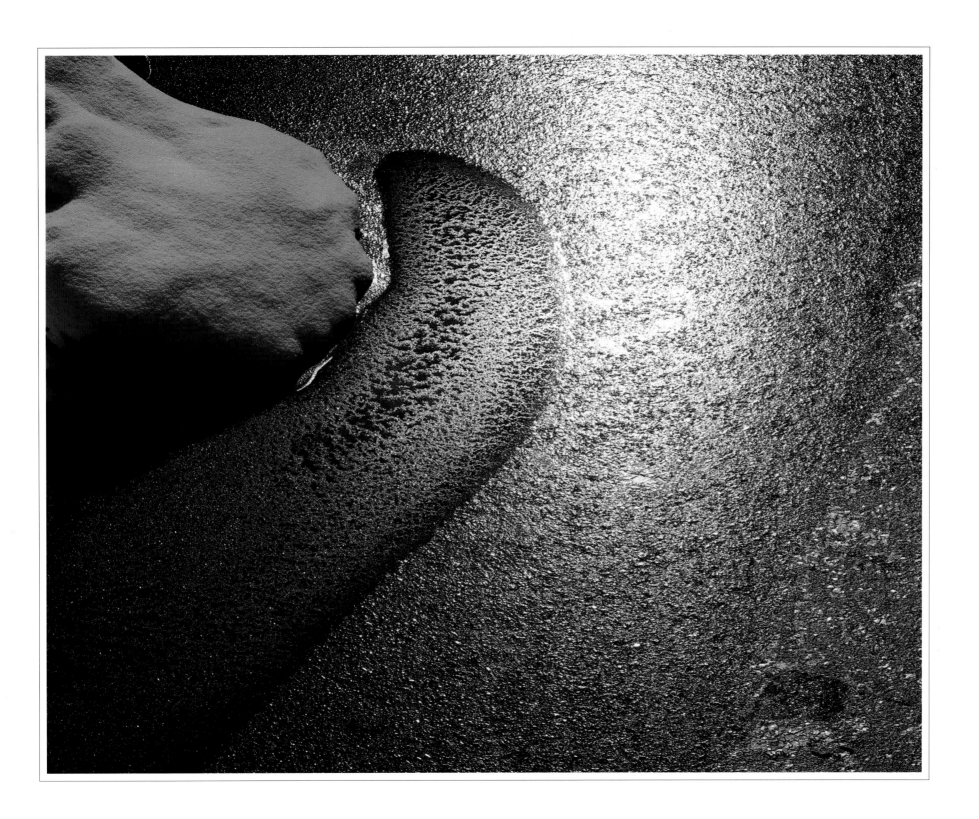

凍る大入川 ◇ この付近は寒さが厳しいため、流れている川の表面が凍ることがある。折しも昇った朝日を受けて、凍った川面は異様な光を放っていた。豊根村

The Onyu River. Its frozen surface is a sparkling fantasy in the light of the newly-risen sun.

寒山遥か ◇ 今朝の冷え込みで茶臼山一帯の樹林にびっしりと霧氷が付いた。気温が上がらぬせいか、冬の日が西に傾くまで梢は霧氷の衣をまとっていた。豊根村

Rime covered branches form a bright spidery pattern against a background of distance mountains.

夜明けの雑木林 ◇ 茶臼山の牧場の中に小さな池がある。池畔に暗いうちから座り込んで夜明けを待った。東の空を赤く染めて、また今日も新しい一日が始まった。豊根村

A forest of mixed hardwoods mirrored in a pond dyed by the rising sun.

奥三河略図　Sketch Map of Okumikawa

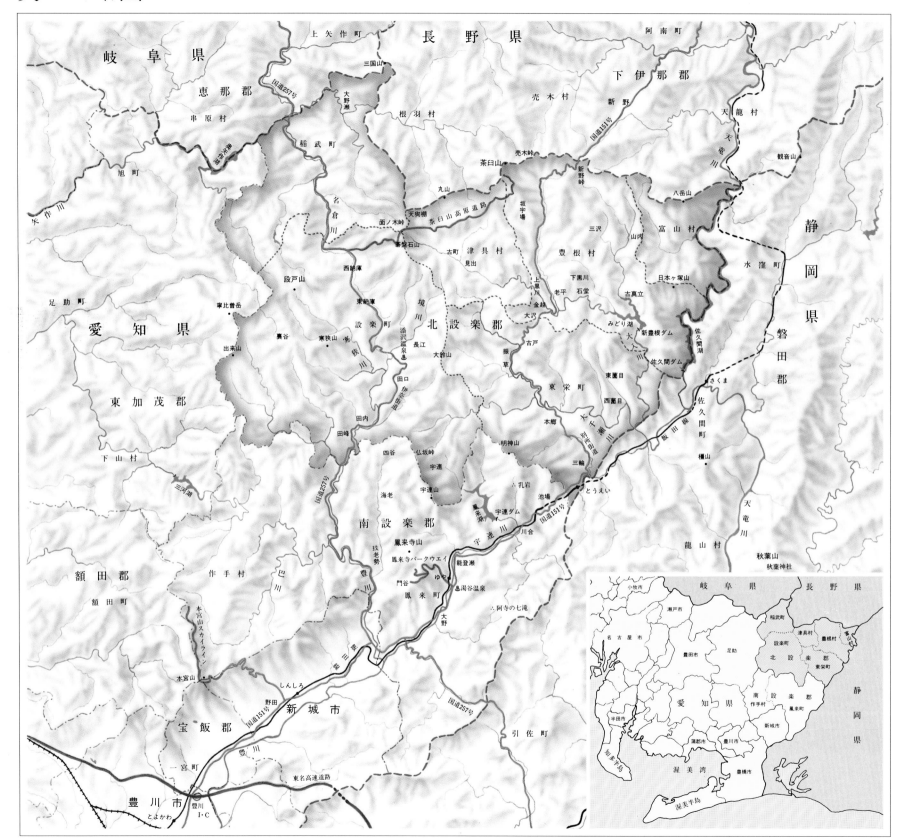

Illustration : Keiji Terakoshi

SPRING AND SUMMER

5——HASSELBLAD 500C/M DISTAGON 60mm F3.5 f11 1sec.

6——TOYO FIELD 4x5 FUJINON 600mm F11 f32 1sec.

7——LINHOF SUPER TECHNIKA 4x5 NIKKOR 150mm F5.6 f22 1/15

8——HASSELBLAD 500C/M SONNAR 250mm F5.6 f32 1/4

9——LINHOF SUPER TECHNIKA 4x5 TELE-XENAR 360mm F5.5 f32 1/2

10——LINHOF SUPER TECHNIKA 4x5 NIKKOR 210mm F5.6 f22 1/15

11——LINHOF SUPER TECHNIKA 4x5 FUJINON 400mm F8 f16 1/30

12——HASSELBLAD 500C/M SONNAR 250mm F5.6 f22 1/15

13——LINHOF SUPER TECHNIKA 4x5 FUJINON 400mm F8 f22 1/8

14——LINHOF SUPER TECHNIKA 4x5 NIKKOR 150mm F5.6 f22 1/15

15——LINHOF SUPER TECHNIKA 4x5 FUJINON 250mm F6.3 f22 1/60

16——LINHOF SUPER TECHNIKA 4x5 FUJINON 400mm F8 f32 1sec.

17——LINHOF SUPER TECHNIKA 4x5 FUJINON 400mm F8 f32 1/8

18——LINHOF SUPER TECHNIKA 4x5 NIKKOR 210mm F5.6 f32 1/4

19——TOYO FIELD 8x10 FUJINON 600mm F11 f16 1/30

20——HASSELBLAD SWC BIOGON 38mm F4.5 f22 1/8

21——LINHOF SUPER TECHNIKA 4x5 SUPER-ANGULON 90mm F8 f32 1/4

22——HASSELBLAD 500C/M PLANAR 100mm F3.5 f11 1/30

23——LINHOF SUPER TECHNIKA 4x5 TELE-XENAR 360mm F5.5 f11 1/15(WITH S.F.FIL.)

24——LINHOF SUPER TECHNIKA 4x5 FUJINON 400mm F8 f32 1/4

25——LINHOF SUPER TECHNIKA 4x5 FUJINON 400mm F8 f32 1/4

26——TOYO FIELD 8x10 FUJINON 300mm F5.6 f45 1/2

27——TOYO FIELD 8x10 FUJINON 600mm F11 f45 1/2

28——HASSELBLAD 500C/M PLANAR 100mm F3.5 f22 1/8

29——LINHOF SUPER TECHNIKA 4x5 TELE-XENAR 360mm F5.5 f22 1/4

30——TOYO FIELD 4x5 FUJINON 600mm F11 f45 1/4

31——LINHOF SUPER TECHNIKA 4x5 FUJINON 125mm F5.6 f22 1/15

32——LINHOF SUPER TECHNIKA 4x5 FUJINON 400mm F8 f16 1/30

33——LINHOF SUPER TECHNIKA 4x5 SUPER-ANGULON 90mm F8 f16 1sec.

34——LINHOF SUPER TECHNIKA 4x5 FUJINON 250mm F6.3 f22 1/15

35——HASSELBLAD 500C/M SONNAR 150mm F4 f8 1/60

36——LINHOF SUPER TECHNIKA 4x5 NIKKOR 150mm F5.6 f22 1/15

37——HASSELBLAD 500C/M SONNAR 150mm F4 f16 1/30

38——LINHOF SUPER TECHNIKA 4x5 FUJINON 400mm F8 f11 30sec.

39——LINHOF SUPER TECHNIKA 4x5 NIKKOR 150mm F5.6 f5.6 5sec.

AUTUMN AND WINTER

45——HASSELBLAD 500C/M SONNAR 250mm F5.6 f22 1/15

46——LINHOF SUPER TECHNIKA 4x5 NIKKOR 210mm F5.6 f22 1/8

47——LINHOF SUPER TECHNIKA 4x5 NIKKOR 210mm F5.5 f22 1/15

48——HASSELBLAD SWC BIOGON 38mm F4.5 f22 1/15

49——HASSELBLAD SWC BIOGON 38mm F4.5 f22 1/4

50·51——TOYO FIELD 8x10 NIKKOR 210mm F5.6 f22 6sec.

52——HASSELBLAD SWC BIOGON 38mm F4.5 f16 1/60

53——LINHOF SUPER TECHNIKA 4x5 FUJINON 400mm F8 f22 1/30

54——TOYO FIELD 8x10 FUJINON 300mm F5.6 f45 1/2

55——TOYO FIELD 4x5 FUJINON 600mm F11 f32 1/8

56——HASSELBLAD 500C/M SONNAR 150mm F4 f22 1/8

57——LINHOF SUPER TECHNIKA 4x5 NIKKOR 210mm F5.6 f32 1/2

58——HASSELBLAD 500C/M SONNAR 150mm F4 f16 1/30

59——HASSELBLAD 500C/M SONNAR 150mm F4 f16 1/30

60——LINHOF SUPER TECHNIKA 4x5 FUJINON 400mm F8 f22 1/30

61——HASSELBLAD 500C/M SONNAR 250mm F5.6 f22 1/30

62——HASSELBLAD 500C/M SONNAR 250mm F5.6 f32 1/2

63——LINHOF SUPER TECHNIKA 4x5 NIKKOR 150mm F5.6 f22 1/15

64——LINHOF SUPER TECHNIKA 4x5 TELE-XENAR 360mm F5.5 f8 1/60

65——LINHOF SUPER TECHNIKA 4x5 TELE-XENAR 360mm F5.5 f16 1/8

66——LINHOF SUPER TECHNIKA 4x5 NIKKOR 210mm F5.6 f22 1/8

67——HASSELBLAD 500C/M TELE-TESSAR 500mm F8 f22 1/4

68——LINHOF SUPER TECHNIKA 4x5 FUJINON 250mm F6.3 f32 1/4

69——LINHOF SUPER TECHNIKA 4x5 FUJINON 250mm F6.3 f22 1sec.

70——TOYO FIELD 8x10 FUJINON 300mm F5.6 f45 1/2

71——HASSELBLAD 500C/M DISTAGON 60mm F3.5 f5.6 1sec.

72——LINHOF SUPER TECHNIKA 4x5 FUJINON 250mm F6.3 f32 1/4

73——LINHOF SUPER TECHNIKA 4x5 FUJINON 400mm F8 f32 1/2

74·75——TOYO FIELD 8x10 FUJINON 600 F11 f32 1/4

76——LINHOF SUPER TECHNIKA 4x5 TELE-XENAR 360mm F5.5 f22 1/8

77——LINHOF SUPER TECHNIKA 4x5 TELE-XENAR 360mm F5.5 f32 1/4

78——LINHOF SUPER TECHNIKA 4x5 NIKKOR 210mm F5.6 f22 1sec.

79——LINHOF SUPER TECHNIKA 4x5 NIKKOR 210mm F5.6 f22 1/4

80——LINHOF SUPER TECHNIKA 4x5 SUPER-ANGULON 90mm F8 f32 1sec.

81——LINHOF SUPER TECHNIKA 4x5 FUJINON 400mm F8 f22 1sec.

82——HASSELBLAD 500C/M TELE-TESSAR 500mm F8 f22 1sec.

83——LINHOF SUPER TECHNIKA 4x5 FUJINON 400mm F8 f32 1/2

84——LINHOF SUPER TECHNIKA 4x5 FUJINON 400mm F8 f22 1/2

85——HASSELBLAD 500C/M DISTAGON 60mm F3.5 f11 1/60

86——LINHOF SUPER TECHNIKA 4x5 SUPER-ANGULON 90mm F8 f22 1/15

87——LINHOF SUPER TECHNIKA 4x5 FUJINON 400mm F8 f22 1/15

88——TOYO FIELD 4x5 FUJINON 600mm F11 f22 1/15

89——LINHOF SUPER TECHNIKA 4x5 FUJINON 400mm F8 f22 1/30

90——LINHOF SUPER TECHNIKA 4x5 FUJINON 125mm F5.6 f16 1/8

91——HASSELBLAD SWC BIOGON 38mm F4.5 f8 1sec.

FILM——EKTACHROME

FUJICHROME

あとがき

前田真三

奥三河がどの辺にあってどのようなところであるかを正確に知る人は少ない。私自身も数年前まで奥三河に対する知識が殆んどなかったといって
よい。行政的には奥三河という呼称はなく、通常、東三河または愛知県東北部と呼ばれている。また、天竜奥三河国定公園という呼名があるが、
これには天竜川流域のかなり広い地域が含まれていて、どの部分までが奥三河であるのか、これとても明確に知る人は少ない。ではどの辺を奥三
河と呼ぶかというと、主に愛知県北設楽郡の設楽町、東栄町、稲武町、豊根村、津具村、富山村などの六ヵ町村を指す場合が多く、さらに隣接地
の足助町、鳳来町、作手村、新城市などの一部も含めて奥三河と呼ぶ場合もあるようである。さて、私が始めて奥三河を訪れたのは、かれこれ十
五年も前のことである。信州の飯田から愛知県の豊橋方面に出るためであった。その後も時折、奥三河を通過した記憶があるが、その頃は文字通
り通り抜けてゆくことだけが目的であったから、悪路だけが印象に残っていて、平凡な山村風景に特に心をひかれるということはなかった。それ
は、当時の私はまだ年齢的にも若く、単に眼に見える現象ばかりを追い求めていた時代であったからかも知れない。

今から十年程前、偶然のことから奥三河の名家熊谷家の当主である熊谷賢一氏と知り合ったことが機縁となって、次第に数多く通うようになって
いった。そうこうしているうちに今まで全く見ばえのしないと思っていた奥三河の風景が、非常に新鮮なものに見えるようになってきた。それは、
そこに日本の山村風景の原点のようなものが潜んでいることを感じとったからである。私のふるさとは東京の西のはずれの山村である。今は都市
化の波に呑まれてしまった感じであるが、かつては素朴な山村であった。そして野鳥を追って山野をかけ廻っていた少年の頃の、心の中にあるふ
るさとの原風景のようなものが、奥三河の風景と接しているうちに、呼び起こされたような気がしている。通えば通う程にその良さがわかってき
て、次第に奥三河に通う回数も増えていった。特にこの二年間は、前記熊谷さんの別宅を借り受けて、そこに住み込んで取材する程に熱も高まっ
ていった。この写真集の出版を誰よりも待ちのぞんでいた筈の熊谷さんは、先頃全く突然に他界されてしまった。私にとっては何ともやりきれな
い気持でいっぱいである。ここに熊谷賢一さんの御冥福を御祈りすると共に、改めて心から感謝の言葉を捧げるものである。

尚、この写真集を飾るにふさわしい文章を頂戴した色川大吉先生をはじめ、御協力頂いた多くの方々に厚く御礼申し上げる次第である。

AFTERWORD

Shinzo Maeda

Not many people know the exact location of Okumikawa or even what kind of place it is, and I myself had hardly any knowledge of this area until several years ago. There is no place called Okumikawa listed in any official administrative district. The area is usually called Eastern Mikawa or simply the northeast part of Aichi Prefecture. There is a Tenryu-Okumikawa Quasi-National Park, but this includes a large area along the Tenryu River which is outside the real Okumikawa. So when one mentions Okumikawa, few people really know what area is being talked about.

Then where is Okumikawa? Well, some people say it is the towns and villages of Shitara, Toei, Inabu, Toyone, Tsugu and Tomiyama; others include Asuke, Horai, Tsukude and Shinshiro.

I first passed through the area about fifteen years ago while on my way to Toyohashi in Aichi from Iida in Nagano Prefecture. In subseqeunt years I occasionally travelled through the area on other trips, but since I was only passing through, I didn't pay much attention except to note that the roads were terrible. Perhaps it was my youth, but I found little to attract me in what seemed at the time to be uninspiring landscapes and ordinary mountain villages.

But about ten years ago I happened to meet Mr. Kenichi Kumagai, the head of the distinguished Kumagai family of Okumikawa, and through him I had several opportunities to revisit the area. I found myself gradually becoming interested in that same scenery which had once seemed plain and unattractive. Perhaps it was because at this time I came to sense something original, the characteristic charm of the Japanese countryside. My own boyhood was spent in a small town west of the Tokyo metropolitan area, and though it has greatly changed over the years, it was once a simple mountain village. In Okumikawa I found a place that brought nostalgic memories of my hometown and those days when, as a country boy, I chased wild birds through the fields. The more I visited Okumikawa, the more I was attracted to it, and my visits to the region became more frequent. For the last two years I have rented part of the Kumagai house and become almost a resident of the area.

I feel deep sorrow in noting here that Mr. Kumagai suddenly passed away just before the publication of this book which he had so eagerly awaited. I sincerely cherish the memory of Kenichi Kumagai and I am thankful for what he did for me. I would also like to express my sincere gratitude to Mr. Daikichi Irokawa who wrote the main text for this book and to the many people who helped bring the work to completion.

前田真三 略歴
BIOGRAPHY——SHINZO MAEDA

1922 ● 東京都八王子市下恩方町に生まれる
Born in Shimo-Ongata-cho, Hachioji City, Tokyo

1948 ● ニチメン㈱に入社、以後17年間つとめる
Employed by Nichimen Co., Ltd.
Works there for the next 17 years

1967 ● フォト・エージェンシー㈱丹溪を設立、代表となる
同時に写真活動に入る
Founds Tankei Photo Agency Co., Ltd., becomes it's representative
Becomes a professional photographer

1974 ● 写真集『ふるさとの四季』(毎日新聞社)
Publishes ''The Four Seasons of a Home Town'' (The Mainichi Newspapers)

1976 ● 写真集『日本の彩』(旅行読売出版社)
写真集『ふるさとの山河』(毎日新聞社)
Publishes ''The Colors of Japan'' (Ryoko Yomiuri Publishing Co.)
Publishes ''Mountains and Rivers of a Home Town'' (The Mainichi Newspapers)

1977 ● 写真集『出合の瞬間』(毎日新聞社)
Publishes ''The Moment of Encounter'' (The Mainichi Newspapers)

1978 ● 写真集『春夏秋冬』(国際情報社)
フォトキナ(西ドイツ・ケルン)に出展
Publishes ''Spring, Summer, Autumn and Winter'' (Kokusai Johosha Publishing Co.)
Exhibits at Fotokina (Köln, West Germany)

1980 ● ユーロ・フォト(スペイン・マジョルカ島)に出展
Exhibits at Europhoto (Majorca, Spain)

1981 ● 写真集『北海道——大地の詩』(集英社)
Publishes ''Hokkaido—Poetry of the Earth'' (Shueisha Publishing Co.)

1982 ● 写真集『山河有情』(保育社)
Publishes ''Scenes from Nature'' (Hoikusha Publishing Co.)

1983 ● 写真集『一木一草』(グラフィック社)
写真集『昭和写真全仕事・前田真三』(朝日新聞社)
Publishes ''A Tree, A Blade of Grass'' (Graphic-sha Publishing Co.)
Publishes ''Shinzo Maeda'' (Asahi Shimbun Publishing Co.)

1984 ● 写真集『上高地』(グラフィック社)
写真集『ランドスケープ・フォトグラフィー』(共著 アメリカ・アムフォト)
写真展『一木一草』(西ドイツ・ハンブルグ 9月、フランス・パリ'85年2月)
日本写真協会年度賞を受賞
Publishes ''The Nippon Alps, Kamikochi'' (Graphic-sha Publishing Co.)
Participates the book,''Landscape Photography'' (Amphoto, U.S.A.)
Holds the exhibition ''A Tree, A Blade of Grass'' (in Hamburg, West Germany on September,
also in Paris, France, on February, 1985)
Receives the Annual Award for the Photographic Socitey of Japan.)

そのほか、日本国内では写真展を10数回開催
Shinzo Maeda has held many photo exhibitions in Japan, in addition to Participating the exhibits listed above.

office ● 株式会社丹溪 〒107 東京都港区北青山2-7-26 メゾン青山402 TEL (03)405-1681
TANKEI CO., LTD. 402 MAISON AOYAMA 2-7-26 KITA-AOYAMA MINATO-KU TOKYO 〒107 PHONE (03)405-1681

奥三河
撮影 前田真三
OKUMIKAWA
Photographed by Shinzo Maeda
1985年6月3日 初版第一刷発行
定価●3,800円 乱丁・落丁はお取替えいたします。

発 行 者●久世利郎
発 行 所●株式会社グラフィック社
　　　　　〒102 東京都千代田区九段北1-9-12 PHONE 03-263-4318
製作協力●フォトライブラリー㈱丹溪
印　　刷●凸版印刷株式会社
製　　本●凸版製本株式会社
写　　植●石井企画